BRAIN OF THRONES
A GAME OF THRONES
QUIZ BOOK

RICH JEPSON
UNOFFICIAL & UNAUTHORIZED

Quiz Books by Rich Jepson

Brain of Thrones: A Game of Thrones Quiz Book

Examinate: A Doctor Who Quiz Book

Harry Swotter: A Harry Potter Quiz Book

Quiz My Face: An Alan Partridge Quiz Book

Riddle Earth: A Lord of the Rings Quiz Book

The Walking Egghead: A Walking Dead Quiz Book

Wisenberg: A Breaking Bad Quiz Book

Brain of Thrones: A Game of Thrones Quiz Book

INTRODUCTION

From Castle Black to Storm's End, Slaver's Bay to Dragonstone, *Game of Thrones* is full of weird and wonderful characters, places and stories.

Now approaching its final season, the HBO drama continues to break boundaries and entertain millions of viewers worldwide.

So how much do you actually know about the TV series? Do you know your Dornish from your Dothraki? Your Tullys from your Tyrells? Your Wildlings from your White Walkers?

Brain of Thrones has been created for fans of the series to test their wits against. Inside this book you will find 25 quizzes consisting of 15 questions each, questions become increasingly difficult as you advance through the book. There are 15 general knowledge rounds and 10 rounds based on specific subjects or themes.

There's also a round of tiebreakers designed to help you figure out who really knows the most about *Game of Thrones*. There's also a round of tiebreakers to settle any disputes, after all...when you play the *Brain of Thrones* – You Win or You Cry!

Contents

QUESTIONS

QUIZ 1 - GENERAL KNOWLEDGE

1. What is the name of the series of novels which *Game of Thrones* is adapted from?

2. Who wrote the novels that *Game of Thrones* is adapted from?

3. In which year did *Game of Thrones* first premier?

4. Who plays the role of Eddard 'Ned' Stark?

5. Which character is only capable of saying their name repeatedly?

6. Which character is commonly referred to as Kingslayer?

7. What is the name of the seat of power that the King or Queen sits on?

8. What animals are used to send messages within the realm?

9. Who fights for Tyrion in his trial by combat in Season 1?

10. Which singer makes a cameo appearance as a Lannister solider in the episode Dragonstone?

11. In Season 1, who is the leader of the Dothraki Horde?

12. Who was the Master of Whisperers on the King's Small Council until he is forced to flee King's Landing?

13. What network produces *Game of Thrones*?

14. How many Kingdoms are there in the known world?

15. How many direwolf pups do the Starks find in the first episode?

Answers - Page 68

QUIZ 2 - GENERAL KNOWLEDGE

1. Who was supposed to escort Jaime Lannister to King's Landing?

2. What is the name of Sansa Stark's direwolf?

3. Who saved Jaime Lannister from Drogon's bolt of fire after he tried to kill Daenerys?

4. Who is Joffrey's biological father?

5. What does the brotherhood of the Night's Watch protect?

6. What is the name of Daenerys Targaryen's power hungry brother?

7. Who declares that they have brought Ice and Fire together in relation to the meeting of Daenerys and Jon Snow?

8. What is the name of the wilding girl that falls in love with Jon Snow?

9. Where in Westeros would you find the Moon Door?

10. Who is Cersei betrothed to marry by her father Tywin?

11. Which of Jaime Lannister's hands gets cut off?

12. Which character does Kit Harington play?

13. Who is Ramsay Snow's father?

14. Who saves Jon from the wights by giving him a horse and sacrificing himself?

15. What name is Petyr Baelish more commonly known by?

Answers - Page 69

QUIZ 3 - General Knowledge

1. What is the name of Sansa Stark's direwolf?

2. Which character receives a large scar across their face during the Battle of the Blackwater?

3. What is the name of the youngest of the Stark siblings?

4. Who succeeds Robert Baratheon as King?

5. Which character does Lena Headey play?

6. Which character is responsible for the torturing and castrating of Theon Greyjoy?

7. What animal is Brienne thrown into a pit with and forced to fight against using only a wooden sword?

8. What three-word phrase does Daenerys say when she returns to Dragonstone?

9. When the Unsullied lay siege to Casterly Rock, where does Jaime deploy the Lannister army to?

10. Who gave Arya her sword?

11. Who marries King Joffrey in Season 3?

12. What was the name of the first ever episode of *Game of Thrones*?

13. What is the name of the law-enforcement institution charged with acting as policemen for King's Landing?

14. Where does Tyrion's first trial by combat take place?

15. What is the name of the actress that plays Arya Stark?

Answers - Page 70

QUIZ 4 - GENERAL KNOWLEDGE

1. Who created the white walkers by stabbing a man with dragonglass?

2. Who does Jamie Lannister attempt to appoint as his general in the episode Stormborn?

3. What is Gendry's profession?

4. Who is responsible for melting down Ned Stark's sword to forge two new swords in Season 4?

5. What does Khal Drogo give Daenerys as a wedding gift?

6. Who succeeds Joffrey as King following his death?

7. What is the name of Theon Greyjoy's sister?

8. Which of the Stark children has a direwolf called Nymeria?

9. Which character does Peter Dinklage play?

10. Which character is renamed 'Reek' after being physically & psychologically tortured?

11. How many daughters does Oberyn Martell have?

12. What is the nickname of Olenna Tyrell?

13. Who informs Arya that Jon Snow is now King of the North?

14. What nickname is Sandor Clegane more commonly known by?

15. Which castle does Bronn ask Jaime Lannister for as payment for his service?

Answers - Page 71

QUIZ 5 - GENERAL KNOWLEDGE

1. What does Ser Loras give to Sansa Stark at the jousting tournament?

2. What is the full name of the character commonly called 'Greatjon'?

3. What 'colour' is associated with King Joffrey's wedding ceremony?

4. Who shot Drogon in his right shoulder with a scorpion bolt?

5. Who publically executes Ser Rodrik Cassel during the fall of Winterfell?

6. What is the name of Joffrey's sister?

7. What is Oberyn Martell's nickname?

8. Which character, along with his followers, is murdered by The Brotherhood without Banners in "The Broken Man'?

9. Who is known as the 'Red Woman'?

10. Who is the commanding officer of the Unsullied?

11. What gift does Littlefinger give Bran?

12. What is the name given to characters that have the ability to enter the minds of animals?

13. Where do Sansa and Arya reunite in Winterfell?

14. Who is Gendry's real father?

15. What does Brienne name the sword Jaime gives her?

Answers - Page 72

QUIZ 6 - ANAGRAMS

Solve each of the following anagrams to find the name of a *Game of Thrones* character:

1. ELF IN GLITTER

2. ARK ASTRAY

3. ENJOY THE GORY

4. NORTHEAST NAB A SIN

5. MAYORS SWAN

6. RAN AS TASKS

7. ALERT MY WALLS

8. INSTANTLY IRONER

9. NORTH BEEF TRAIN

10. ANGER RAN YESTERDAY

11. LOOSEN TO ROB

12. EL NOBLE MARTYR

13. RED TANKS

14. BREATHER ONTO BAR

15. RETAIN SILENCERS

16. NORTH MOOR JAM

17. A WOODS HARVEST

18. GYM ROWER

19. ANIMAL IN JESTER

20. OH ROD, OH ROD, OH ROD

Answers - Page 73

QUIZ 7 - THE STARKS

1. Who does Arya execute with a Valyrian dagger on the order of Sansa?

2. What is the motto of House Stark?

3. What is the name of Arya Stark's sword?

4. Which character pushed Bran Stark from a tower, causing him to suffer a crippling injury?

5. Where is the Seat of House Stark?

6. What role does Robert Baratheon offer Ned Stark?

7. Which of the Stark siblings has a direwolf called Grey Wind?

8. What is the name of Ned Stark's Valyrian steel sword that he uses to perform an execution in the opening episode?

9. Which character is known for carrying Bran on his back?

10. What creature, with a distinguishing feature, does Brandon Stark have a recurring dream about?

11. How many years did Theon Greyjoy spend living as a ward of the Starks?

12. What crime was Eddard Stark put on trial for?

13. What is the name of the wildling girl who travels with Bran to The Wall?

14. Who does Robb Stark marry?

15. What name does Arya call herself when she is disguised as an orphan boy in Season 2?

Answers - Page 74

QUIZ 8 - THE KNOWN WORLD

1. What are the names of the two continents where the story takes place?

2. Where is Castle Black located?

3. Which Bay does King's Landing overlook?

4. What is the name of the slum in King's Landing?

5. Which Islands are home to House Greyjoy?

6. What is the name of the sea that lies North of Braavos?

7. Where would you find the Warden of the West?

8. Where would you find the ancestral seat of House Targaryen?

9. Where does the 'Red Wedding' take place?

10. Whose Keep lies beyond The Wall?

11. Which mountaintop fortress locks its criminals in three-walled 'sky cells'?

12. What are the names of the three cities Daenerys visits along the coast of Slaver's Bay?

13. What is the name of the vast, barren desert that lays to the east of the Dothraki Sea?

14. Which region is Loras Tyrell from?

15. Which sea separates the two main continents?

Answers - Page 75

QUIZ 9 - MOTHER OF DRAGONS

1. Whilst pregnant, what does Daenerys Targaryen eat to prove herself to the Dothraki people?

2. Who is Ser Jorah working for as a spy when he first encounters Daenerys?

3. How many men does Daenerys send to open the front gates of Yunkai?

4. What is the name of the leader of the Second Sons, who kills his superiors in order to align with Daenerys?

5. What is inside a ball given to Daenerys by a young girl in the first episode of Season 3?

6. By what nickname is the city of Yunkai also known?

7. Who serves as Daenerys' handmaiden and advisor in the third Season?

8. What does Daenerys call her horse?

9. Which city are Daenerys and her brother in exile at the beginning of the first Season?

10. Who receives Daenerys at the gates of Qarth?

11. What is the name of Daenerys' army that she purchases from a slave trader in Astapor?

12. What is the name of the house where Pyat Pree holds Daenerys' dragons captive?

13. What kind of merchant tries to assassinate Daenerys in the marketplace?

14. Who performs a curse on Khal Drogo?

15. What is the name of the servant who betrays Daenerys to Xaro Xoan Daxos?

Answers - Page 76

QUIZ 10 - NOBLE HOUSES

Name each of the following Houses from the description of their flags below:

1. A crowned black stag rampant on a gold background

2. A three-headed dragon on a black background

3. A golden lion rampant on a crimson background

4. A red sun pierced by a gold spear on an orange background

5. A grey direwolf on a white background (sometimes with pale green as well)

6. Two stone grey towers and connecting bridge over water on a dark grey background

7. A gold rose on a green background

8. A silver trout leaping on a red and blue background

9. A white falcon and crescent moon on a blue background

10. A red flayed man, hanging upside down on a white X-shaped cross, on a black background

Can you name each of the following Houses from their 'words' below?

1. Family, Duty, Honor

2. Growing Strong

3. We Do Not Sow

4. Ours Is The Fury

5. As High As Honor

6. Fire And Blood

7. Hear Me Roar

8. Unbowed, Unbent, Unbroken

9. Our blades are sharp

10. We stand together

Answers - Page 77

QUIZ 11 - GENERAL KNOWLEDGE

1. Which character is wounded following a wight bear attack beyond The Wall?

2. Which actor plays the role of Archmaester Ebrose?

3. Who is known as 'The Onion Knight'?

4. Where does Tyrion attempt to send Shae after she is discovered?

5. What does 'Valar Morghulis' translate to in English?

6. Which three characters serve as judges at Tyrion's trial?

7. Who is appointed Warden of the North after the events of the 'Red Wedding'?

8. Who is Gendry's father?

9. What do Pyromancers make?

10. What phrase is the name 'Hodor' an abbreviation of?

11. Who dies as the result of having molten gold symbolically poured over their head?

12. How many swords is the Iron Throne forged from?

13. What creature decorates the fireplace in Balon Greyjoy's hall?

14. Who turns Gendry over to Melisandre?

15. What job did Hodor have in Winterfell?

Answers - Page 78

QUIZ 12 - GENERAL KNOWLEDGE

1. Who kills Balon Greyjoy?

2. How did Tywin Lannister's wife die?

3. What phrase do wildings use to describe red haired characters, such as Ygritte?

4. Who was hand of the King to Robert Baratheon before Ned Stark?

5. What is the name of the wildling that has the ability to warg into his Eagle?

6. Which character does Lady Crane play in the Braavosi theatre troupe?

7. What is the name of Lysa & Jon Arryn's son?

8. What is the name of the poison Cersei uses to kill Tyene in front of her mother?

9. Which dragon does Jon Snow pet after Daenerys returns from battle?

10. What was the name of Arya Stark's sword instructor?

11. Who is named captain of the City Watch after Robert Baratheon dies?

12. What type of animal kills Robert Baratheon?

13. What was the name of the woman that Tyrion married when he was young?

14. What is the name of the first character to die in *Game of Thrones*?

15. Whose head does Joffrey also put on a spike next to Ned Stark?

Answers - Page 79

QUIZ 13 - GENERAL KNOWLEDGE

1. What is the name of Jon Snow's Valyrian steel sword?

2. Which symbolic items does Daenerys Targaryen catapult against the walls of Meereen?

3. Whilst in Robb Stark's captivity, Jaime Lannister finds himself in company with his distant cousin. What is his name?

4. What substance does Tyrion Lannister use to defeat Stannis Baratheon at the Battle of Blackwater?

5. Which character does Catelyn Stark notice wearing armour beneath his outfit at the 'Red Wedding'?

6. What is the name of the God Melisandre worships?

7. What kind of poison is used to assassinate King Joffrey?

8. Who is the leader of the Brotherhood without Banners?

9. Which dragon does the Night King kill with a spear and later reanimate?

10. Which two characters were getting married prior to the 'Red Wedding' massacre?

11. What is Jon Snow's true name?

12. When they were children, why did Gregor Clegane burn his brother's face?

13. What are the Faceless Men a guild of?

14. What is the name of the huge weapon that the Night's Watch drop across the face of The Wall to stop the wildlings?

15. Who smuggles Gendry out of Dragonstone in a rowboat?

Answers - Page 80

Quiz 14 - General Knowledge

1. What is the name of the captain of the guards at The Eyrie, who Bronn kills in Tyrion's trial by combat?

2. Who is Catelyn Stark's father?

3. Who does Gendry give his war hammer to before running back to Eastwatch?

4. Which character is known as The Little Lion?

5. Who gives Daenerys three dragon eggs as a wedding gift?

6. What is the name of Stannis Baratheon's flagship that leads the attack during the Battle of the Blackwater?

7. Which sellsword company does Cersei plan to hire to bolster the Lannister army?

8. Which Isle does Jaime Lannister tell Locke that Brienne is the sole heiress of?

9. What is the name of the pirate-lord that Stannis Baratheon recruits after securing a loan at the Iron Bank?

10. What type of tree do new members of the Night's Watch swear their vows before?

11. At which castle does Arya Stark become Tywin Lannister's cupbearer?

12. What is the name of Ned Stark's younger brother, who is also First Ranger of the Night's Watch?

13. What is the name of the desert surrounding the city of Qarth?

14. What is the name of the giant who attacks the Night's Watch through the inner gate?

15. Where does Meera tell Bran she is returning to before leaving Winterfell?

Answers - Page 81

QUIZ 15 - GENERAL KNOWLEDGE

1. Who does Petyr Baelish push out of the moon door?

2. What is The Hound's biggest fear?

3. What is "Tears of Lys"?

4. What is the name of Stannis Baratheon's only daughter?

5. In which city would you find the Iron Bank?

6. Which birds were placed inside the ceremonial pie at the Joffrey's wedding?

7. What is the name of the castle that Theon Greyjoy is held captive in whilst he is being tortured?

8. What is the name of the only wildling to survive the rear assault on Castle Black?

9. What is the name of the song dedicated to House Lannister?

10. What is the name of the prostitute that Joffrey kills with a crossbow?

11. Where do Brienne & The Hound have a fierce battle?

12. Which character asks Arya for three names for him to assassinate?

13. Who does Tormund develop a crush on in Season 6?

14. What is the name of the battle that takes place between the Night's Watch and the White Walkers in Season 2?

15. What food does Davos pretend to be smuggling when questioned by the Gold Cloaks on the shores of Blackwater Bay?

Answers - Page 82

QUIZ 16 - A SONG OF ICE & FIRE

1. What is the name of the first book in the novel series?

2. What is the name of the second book in the novel series?

3. What is the name of the third book in the novel series?

4. What is the name of the forth book in the novel series?

5. What is the name of the fifth book in the novel series?

6. What is the name of the (as yet) unpublished sixth book in the novel series?

7. What is the name of the (as yet) unpublished seventh book in the novel series?

8. When was the first book published?

9. Which J. R. R. Tolkien story is said to have inspired A Song of Ice and Fire?

10. Which 15th century English civil war is said to be a source of inspiration for A Song of Ice and Fire?

11. What nationality is George R. R. Martin?

12. What does the 'R. R.' in George R. R. Martin's name stand for?

13. Which UK landmark did George R. R. Martin say was his inspiration for 'The Wall'?

14. In which decade was George R. R. Martin born?

15. On what device does George R. R. Martin write all of his books?

Answers - Page 83

QUIZ 17 - QUOTES

Name the characters that said each of the following quotes:

1. "A dragon is not a slave"

2. "You know nothing Jon Snow"

3. "When you play the game of thrones, you win or you die"

4. "It's the family name that lives on. That's all that lives on. Not your personal glory, not your honour, but family."

5. "The Lannisters send their regards"

6. "I will not become a page in someone else's history book"

7. "Chaos is a ladder"

8. "War was easier than daughters"

9. "The night is dark and full of terrors"

10. "Your joy will turn to ashes in your mouth"

11. "Someday I'm going to put a sword through your eye and out the back of your skull"

12. "The things I do for love"

13. "I'm simply asking you to run my kingdom while I eat, drink and whore myself into an early grave"

14. "The man who passes the sentence should swing the sword"

15. "A girl gives a man his own name?"

16. "If you think this has a happy ending, you haven't been paying attention"

17. "Wasn't sure I'd find you. Thought you might still be rowing"

18. "I want to make babies with her. Think of them. Great big monsters! They'd conquer the world!"

19. "Drink until it feels like you did the right thing"

20. "I'm gonna light the biggest fire the North has ever seen!"

Answers - Page 84

QUIZ 18 - THE WALL

1. Who is known as the King Beyond The Wall?

2. How many watchtowers lay along The Wall?

3. What colour are the eyes of White Walkers?

4. What are the 'free folk' beyond The Wall commonly referred to as?

5. What is the name of the woodland area that lies directly beyond The Wall?

6. Who is credited with building The Wall?

7. What is the name of the town where Samwell hides Gilly and her baby in order to keep them safe?

8. How long is The Wall approximately?

9. Which watchtower was destroyed by the Night King and his dragon?

10. How old is The Wall approximately?

11. What part of The Wall does Jon recommend be sealed off during the attack on Castle Black?

12. How many of the castles along The Wall are manned?

13. In Season 1, who is the master-at-arms responsible for training new recruits?

14. How tall is The Wall approximately?

15. What is the name of the recruiter for the Night's Watch who meets Jon Snow in Season 1?

Answers - Page 85

QUIZ 19 - THE CAST

1. Which actor quit acting after his time of *Game of Thrones* ended?

2. Which character does Kit Harrington portray in the series?

3. How tall is Brienne of Tarth actress Gwendoline Christie?

4. Which English city was Sean Bean born in?

5. What is the name of the actor who plays Robb Stark?

6. Which notable actor in the show starred in films such Alien3, *The Last Action Hero* & *The Imitation Game*?

7. The actress who plays Talisa Stark is the real-life Granddaughter of which legendary entertainer?

8. Prior to playing the role of Bronn, Jerome Flynn was part of a 90s-pop duo with which other singer?

9. Which *Game of Thrones* actor played the leading role in the 2011 remake of *Conan The Barbarian*?

10. Which actress in the show played the role of Queen Gorgo in *300*?

11. Which Dutch actress plays Melisandre?

12. Which British actress plays Olenna Tyrell?

13. Which 2003 Richard Curtis film did Jojen Reed actor Thomas Brodie-Sangster appear in?

14. Which *Game of Thrones* actress played the role of Margot Al-Harazi in *24: Live Another Day*?

15. What is the name of the real-life sister of the actor who plays Theon Greyjoy?

Answers - Page 86

QUIZ 20 - DEATH

Who killed each of the following characters?

1. Viserys Targaryen

2. Robb Stark

3. Oberyn Martell

4. Lysa Arryn

5. Tywin Lannister

6. Eddard Stark

7. Joffrey Baratheon

8. Stannis Baratheon

9. Lord Commander Mormont

10. Pypar

11. Catelyn Stark

12. Locke

13. Ygritte

14. Ser Rodrick Cassel

15. Khal Drogo

16. Petyr Baelish

17. Rickon Stark

18. Ros

19. Talisa Stark

20. Jon Umber

Answers - Page 87

QUIZ 21 - GENERAL KNOWLEDGE

1. Who was known as 'The Mad King"?

2. What is the nickname of Brynden Tully?

3. What is the name of Oberyn Martell's sister?

4. What is the name of Jon Snow's mother?

5. What is the name of the table in the main hall at the castle of Dragonstone?

6. Which island does Missandei hail from?

7. What is the name of Davos Seaworth's son?

8. What phrase is commonly used during funerals of Night's Watchmen as a mark of respect?

9. What is the name of the girl whose corpse is fed to the hounds by Ramsay Bolton?

10. What is the name of the master of the Citadel who attempts to kill Melisandre by poisoning her cup of wine?

11. Which siege do Thoros of Myr and Jorah Mormont reminisce when they go beyond The Wall?

12. What is the name of Rickon Stark's direwolf?

13. What weapon does Samwell Tarly use to kill a White Walker?

14. Who travels with Catelyn Stark to King's Landing?

15. Who does Khal Drogo assign as Daenerys' bodyguard?

Answers - Page 88

QUIZ 22 - General Knowledge

1. Which character does John Bradley play in the series?

2. What is the name of the butcher's son that Joffrey bullies and Arya tries to save?

3. Who cuts off Jaime Lannister's right hand?

4. What does three blasts on a horn signal for members of the Night's Watch?

5. Who saves Bran and Meera from being attacked by the wights?

6. What is Ser Loras Tyrell's nickname?

7. What was Daenerys Targaryen going to call her baby?

8. Who baptizes Euron Greyjoy?

9. Which dragon forged the seven kingdoms together by fire according to Viserys Targaryen?

10. What was Robert Baratheon's weapon of choice?

11. What is the name of the forest that lies to the north of Winterfell?

12. What is Catelyn Stark's maiden name?

13. What is the name of the Septa who Cersei captures and orders Ser Gregor to torture?

14. What flavour wine does Arya drink with the Lannister soldiers?

15. Which actor plays Tycho Nestoris?

Answers - Page 89

QUIZ 23 - GENERAL KNOWLEDGE

1. What is the nickname of the character that Oberyn Martell faced off against in Tyrion's trial by combat?

2. What is the name of Theon Greyjoy's horse?

3. Who resurrects Beric Dondarrion after his fight with Sandor Clegane?

4. What name did Robb & Talisa Stark choose for their unborn child?

5. Who does Petyr Baelish ask to take him to the safety of the Vale during his trial at Winterfell?

6. What is the name of the sword owned by Prince Joffrey in the first Season?

7. What are Oberyn Martell's daughters collectively known as?

8. Who fails to hit the funeral boat of Lord Hoster Tully three times with flaming arrows?

9. What is the name of the character that is in charge of the Sky Cells at The Eyrie?

10. What is the name of the wildling tribe that shave their heads bald and engage in cannibalism?

11. Where is Ned Stark stabbed during his fight with Jaime Lannister?

12. Which Ironborn raider does Theon have a fight with on the beach at Dragonstone?

13. Who killed Jon Arryn?

14. What is the name of the Valyrian steel blade held by House Tarly?

15. In whose diary does Gilly discover Prince Rhaegar's marriage annulment?

Answers - Page 90

Quiz 24 - General Knowledge

1. What is the nickname of Lord Mormont?

2. Who composed the theme tune to *Game of Thrones*?

3. Who vouches for Daenerys allowing her to gain entry into the city of Qarth?

4. How tall is the Great Pyramid of Meereen?

5. What language do the White Walkers speak?

6. What is the name of the Maester who had previously treated greyscale before Samwell?

7. What is the name of the slave-trader who sells Daenerys the Unsullied?

8. What are the names of the two characters that are being transported in a cage to The Wall alongside Jaqan H'ghar?

9. What are the names of the two swords made from the Valyrian steel original used in Eddard Stark's sword?

10. Who is the leader of the Black Ears hill tribe?

11. Who are Daenerys and her brother staying with at the start of Season 1?

12. What is the name of the slave-trader who asks Daenerys to allow him to bury his father in a temple in Meereen?

13. Who says, "Wise men do not make demands of kings"?

14. What is Hodor's real name?

15. What command does Daenerys give to instruct Drogon to blast a torrent of fire at the Lannister army?

Answers - Page 91

QUIZ 25 - GENERAL KNOWLEDGE

1. Which character has their tongue cut out after singing a song about Robert Baratheon & Cersei Lannister?

2. Who does Gendry apprentice for at Winterfell?

3. Who is the Magnar of Thenn?

4. Which dragon's skull does Cersei fire a bolt through whilst testing a ballista underneath the Red Keep?

5. Where is the seat of House Mormont?

6. How many languages does Missandei claim that she is able to speak?

7. What is the name of the acting Lord Commander of the Knight's watch, who greets Bran at The Wall?

8. Which hill tribe is Shagga the leader of?

9. What is the name of the building in which Margaery and Joffrey have their Royal Wedding?

10. What is the name of the male prostitute who poses as Loras Tyrell's squire when he is actually spying for Petyr Baelish?

11. What is the capital of Dorne?

12. What are the three orders of the Night's Watch?

13. Which country was actor Nikolaj Coster-Waldau born in?

14. Who said, "Most men would rather deny a hard truth than face it"?

15. Who killed Orell?

Answers - Page 92

TIEBREAKERS

Score tied? Whoever has the closest answer to one of the following questions wins the quiz.

1. In the first episode, how long, in minutes and seconds, does it take for the first death to occur?

2. How many characters are beheaded in the first four seasons?

3. How many characters (including extras) have died on *Game of Thrones* so far?

4. How much, in U.S dollars, has *Game of Thrones* brought to Northern Ireland's economy?

5. How many days did it take to shoot "The Battle of the Bastards"?

6. How many died at the Battle of Castle Black?

7. What percentage of *Game of Thrones* viewership is female?

8. In 2012, how many baby girls were named Khaleesi in the U.S?

9. How many viewers tuned in to the *Game of Thrones* premiere episode?

10. How much does the average episode of *Game of Thrones* cost HBO to make in U.S dollars?

Answers - Page 93

ANSWERS

Quiz 1 - Answers

1. A Song of Ice and Fire
2. George R. R. Martin
3. 2011
4. Sean Bean
5. Hodor
6. Jaime Lannister
7. The Iron Throne
8. Ravens
9. Bronn
10. Ed Sheeran
11. Khal Drogo
12. Lord Varys
13. HBO
14. 7
15. 6

Quiz 2 - Answers

1. Brienne of Tarth

2. Lady

3. Bronn

4. Jaime Lannister

5. The Wall

6. Viserys

7. Melisandre

8. Ygritte

9. The Eyrie

10. Ser Loras Tyrell

11. His right hand

12. Jon Snow

13. Roose Bolton

14. Benjen Stark

15. Littlefinger

QUIZ 3 - ANSWERS

1. Lady

2. Tyrion Lannister

3. Rickon Stark

4. Joffrey Baratheon

5. Cersei Lannister

6. Ramsay Snow

7. A bear

8. "Shall we begin?"

9. Highgarden

10. Jon Snow

11. Margaery Tyrell

12. Winter Is Coming

13. The City Watch

14. The Eyrie

15. Maisie Williams

QUIZ 4 - ANSWERS

1. The Children of the Forest

2. Randyll Tarly

3. Blacksmith

4. Tywin Lannister

5. A white horse

6. Tommen Baratheon

7. Yara

8. Arya Stark

9. Tyrion Lannister

10. Theon Greyjoy

11. 8

12. The Queen of Thorns

13. Hot Pie

14. The Hound

15. Highgarden

QUIZ 5 - ANSWERS

1. A red rose

2. Jon Umber

3. Purple

4. Bronn

5. Theon Greyjoy

6. Myrcella Baratheon

7. The Red Viper

8. Brother Ray

9. Melisandre

10. Grey Worm

11. A Valyrian steel dagger

12. Warg

13. In the crypts, overlooking Ned's grave

14. Robert Baratheon

15. Oathkeeper

QUIZ 6 - ANSWERS

1. Littlefinger

2. Arya Stark

3. Theon Greyjoy

4. Stannis Baratheon

5. Ramsay Snow

6. Sansa Stark

7. Samwell Tarly

8. Tyrion Lannister

9. Brienne of Tarth

10. Daenerys Targaryen

11. Roose Bolton

12. Oberyn Martell

13. Ned Stark

14. Robert Baratheon

15. Cersei Lannister

16. Jorah Mormont

17. Davos Seaworth

18. Grey Worm

19. Jaime Lannister

20. Hodor, Hodor, Hodor

QUIZ 7 - ANSWERS

1. Petyr Baelish
2. Winter Is Coming
3. Needle
4. Jaime Lannister
5. Winterfell
6. Hand of the King
7. Robb Stark
8. Ice
9. Hodor
10. Three Eyed Raven
11. 9
12. Treason
13. Osha
14. Talisa Maegyr
15. Arry

Quiz 8 - Answers

1. Westeros & Essos
2. The Wall
3. Blackwater Bay
4. Flea Bottom
5. Iron Islands
6. The Shivering Sea
7. Casterly Rock
8. Dragonstone
9. The Twins
10. Craster's Keep
11. The Eyrie
12. Meereen, Yunkai & Astapor
13. Red Waste
14. Highgarden
15. The Narrow Sea

QUIZ 9 - ANSWERS

1. A raw horse heart
2. Lord Varys
3. 3
4. Daario Naharis
5. A manticore
6. The Yellow City
7. Missandei
8. Silver
9. Pentos
10. The Thirteen
11. The Unsullied
12. House of the Undying
13. A wine merchant
14. Mirri Maz Duur
15. Doreah

QUIZ 10 - ANSWERS

1. House Baratheon
2. House Targaryen
3. House Lannister
4. House Martell
5. House Stark
6. House Frey
7. House Tyrell
8. House Tully
9. House Arryn
10. House Bolton

1. House Tully
2. House Tyrell
3. House Greyjoy
4. House Baratheon
5. House Arryn
6. House Targaryen
7. House Lannister
8. House Martell
9. House Bolton
10. House Frey

Quiz 11 - Answers

1. Thoros of Myr
2. Jim Broadbent
3. Davos Seaworth
4. Pentos
5. All Men Must Die
6. Tywin Lannister, Oberyn Martell & Mace Tyrell
7. Roose Bolton
8. Robert Baratheon
9. Wildfire
10. "Hold the door"
11. Viserys Targaryen
12. 1000
13. Giant Squid
14. The Brotherhood without Banners
15. Stable boy

Quiz 12 - Answers

1. Euron

2. Giving birth to Tyrion

3. 'Kissed By Fire'

4. Jon Arryn

5. Orell

6. Cersei Lannister

7. Robin Arryn

8. Long Farewell

9. Drogon

10. Syrio Forel

11. Janos Slynt

12. A boar

13. Tysha

14. Waymar Royce

15. Septa Mordane

Quiz 13 - Answers

1. Longclaw
2. Broken Chains
3. Alton Lannister
4. Wildfire
5. Roose Bolton
6. The Lord of Light
7. The Strangler
8. Beric Dondarrion
9. Viserion
10. Edmure Tully & Roslyn Frey
11. Aegon Targaryen
12. Because he played with his toy
13. Assassins
14. A scythe
15. Davos Seaworth

Quiz 14 - Answers

1. Ser Vardis Egan
2. Lord Hoster Tully
3. Tormund
4. Tyrion Lannister
5. Illyrio Mopatis
6. The Fury
7. The Golden Company
8. Sapphire Isle
9. Sallandhor Saan
10. Heart Tree
11. Harrenhal
12. Benjen Stark
13. Garden of Bones
14. Mag the Mighty
15. The Neck

QUIZ 15 - ANSWERS

1. Lysa Arryn

2. Fire

3. Poison

4. Shireen

5. Braavos

6. Doves

7. The Dreadfort

8. Tormund Giantsbane

9. The Rains of Castamere

10. Ros

11. The Vale of Arryn

12. Jaqan H'ghar

13. Brienne of Tarth

14. Battle of the Fist of the First Men

15. Fermented Crab

Quiz 16 - Answers

1. A Game of Thrones

2. A Clash of Kings

3. A Storm of Swords

4. A Feast for Crows

5. A Dance with Dragons

6. The Winds of Winter

7. A Dream of Spring

8. 1996

9. The Lord of The Rings

10. The War of the Roses

11. American

12. Raymond Richard

13. Hadrian's Wall

14. 1940s

15. A DOS computer

Quiz 17 - Answers

1. Daenerys Targaryen
2. Ygritte
3. Cersei Lannister
4. Tywin Lannister
5. Roose Bolton
6. Stannis Baratheon
7. Petyr Baelish
8. Ned Stark
9. Melisandre
10. Tyrion Lannister
11. Arya Stark
12. Jaime Lannister
13. Robert Baratheon
14. Ned Stark
15. Jaqen H'ghar
16. Ramsay Snow
17. Davos Seaworth
18. Tormund Wolfsbane
19. Bronn
20. Mance Rayder

Quiz 18 - Answers

1. Mance Rayder

2. 19

3. Blue

4. Wildlings

5. The Haunted Forest

6. Bran the Builder

7. Mole's Town

8. 300 miles

9. Eastwatch

10. 8,000 years old

11. The Tunnel

12. 3

13. Ser Alliser Thorne

14. 700ft

15. Yoren

QUIZ 19 - ANSWERS

1. Jack Gleeson

2. Jon Snow

3. 1.91m / 6 ft. 3 in

4. Sheffield

5. Richard Madden

6. Charles Dance

7. Charlie Chaplin

8. Robson Green

9. Jason Momoa

10. Lena Headey

11. Carice van Houten

12. Diana Rigg

13. Love Actually

14. Michelle Fairley

15. Lily Allen

QUIZ 20 - ANSWERS

1. Khal Drogo
2. Roose Bolton
3. Gregor Clegane
4. Petyr Baelish
5. Tyrion Lannister
6. Ser Ilyn Payne
7. Olenna Tyrell & Petyr Baelish
8. Brienne of Tarth
9. Rast
10. Ygritte
11. Black Walder Rivers
12. Hodor (after Bran warged into him)
13. Olly
14. Theon Greyjoy
15. Daenerys Targaryen
16. Arya Stark
17. Ramsay Bolton
18. Joffrey Baratheon
19. Lothar Frey
20. Tormund Wolfsbane

Quiz 21 - Answers

1. Aerys Targaryen
2. The Blackfish
3. Elia Martell
4. Lyanna Stark
5. The Painted Table
6. Naarth
7. Matthos Seaworth
8. And Now His Watch Is Ended
9. Myranda
10. Cressen
11. The Siege of Pyke
12. Shaggydog
13. A dragonglass dagger
14. Rodrick Cassel
15. Rakharo

QUIZ 22 - ANSWERS

1. Samwell Tarly

2. Mycah

3. Locke

4. White Walkers

5. Benjen Stark

6. Knight of Flowers

7. Rhaego

8. Aeron Greyjoy

9. Balerion

10. War Hammer

11. Wolfswood

12. Tully

13. Septa Unella

14. Blackberry wine

15. Mark Gatiss

Quiz 23 - Answers

1. The Mountain
2. Smiler
3. Thoros of Myr
4. Eddard
5. Yohn Royce
6. Lion's Tooth
7. Sand Snakes
8. Edmure Tully
9. Mord
10. Thenns
11. In his right leg
12. Harrag
13. Lysa Arryn
14. Heartsbane
15. High Septon
    Maynard

QUIZ 24 - ANSWERS

1. The Bear
2. Ramin Djawadi
3. Xaro Xhoan Daxos
4. 800ft
5. Skroth
6. Maestar Pylos
7. Kraznys mo Nakloz
8. Biter & Rorge
9. Oathkeeper & Widow's Wail
10. Chella
11. Illyrio Mopatis
12. Hizdah zo Loraq
13. Catelyn Stark
14. Wylis
15. "Dracarys"

Quiz 25 - Answers

1. Marillion
2. Tobho Mott
3. Styr
4. Balerion the Black Dread
5. Bear Island
6. 19
7. Eddison Tollett
8. The Stone Crows
9. Great Sept of Baelor
10. Olyvar
11. Sunspear
12. Builder, Ranger, Steward
13. Denmark
14. Tyrion Lannister
15. Jon Snow

TIEBREAKER ANSWERS

1. 6m 58s

2. 4

3. 1,243

4. $100million

5. 25

6. 86

7. 42%

8. 146

9. 2.2million

10. $6million

72672131R00057

Made in the USA
Middletown, DE
08 May 2018